CANCER
SAVED
MY SOUL

CANCER SAVED MY SOUL

VALLYRIE SHERIDAN-LANCASTER

Charleston, SC
www.PalmettoPublishing.com

Cancer Saved My Soul

First Edition

Hardcover ISBN: 978-1-68515-861-3
Paperback ISBN: 978-1-68515-466-0
eBook ISBN: 978-1-68515-467-7

*To all cancer patients and patients with diseases known to God.
That means all.*

God knows our weakness and he knows how to get our attention.

*Healing starts with self-forgiveness.
The next step is to forgive others*

Time to get right with God.

It's like a fisherman who is pulling fish in with his fish nets.

*We are the fish, and the net is the disease, pain or illness is the sacrifice and
the fisherman is God.*

God is pulling us in to come back to him.

Cancer saved my life.

This is true. Cancer did save my life. I know what you are thinking. "She done lost her mind." "What is she talking about?" "Cancer is a curse." Cancer took my loved one." "Cancer is killing me." I had all those reactions and thoughts too.

For the lovely people who say cancer took our loved ones. God knows why and he was trying to get your attention. We don't know God, but he knows us and our ways. He knows our weakness. He knows our strength. He knows our motivations. He knows our secrets and sins. His question to us is "Did you get it?"

Remember, God knows our weakness. He is alpha and omega, the beginning and the end. He knew us while or before we were conceived. KJV Genesis 2:7, Jeremiah 1:5

This book is written from my spiritual and personal understanding of why I had cancer and what I had to do to heal it.

God Almighty knew how to make me get right with him. We all have weaknesses and God knows them. We have things hidden in us and only God know what they are. We have done things that were not right and thought that they were forgotten. They were not forgotten. We have made promises to God and broken our contract with him.

My friends, once you read this your mind will open with great wisdom and understanding. I pray you take this and go further and learn your lesson and heal.

Before you read further into this book you must understand I say this again, that this is written from my personal life experiences. I am giving you some of my personal challenges, life experiences and God's wisdom. In return, you will understand how cancer saved my life and the reason I had cancer. This suffering was a physical and spiritual journey. You will see how it led me back to God.

I pray this will help both the victims of cancer and family members who have loved ones who are suffering from cancer and other illnesses. We have lost our way and need to come back to God. I know you can't see the truth, or you may be ignoring it, but God is with you. You need to accept his words again. Become a child of God again.

I start this off where it all began, with my childhood. I had a happy, imaginary, fun and busy life. I loved to fish. I was a creative child and a girl who like to hang out with the boys.

I was born at Kapiolani Hospital and raised in Pearl City, Honolulu and Enchanted Lakes, Kailua. I was a hula dancer and swimmer and a high school athlete with many competitions. Swimming was my sport. I still swim today. Even though I was an athlete I was a private girl. I didn't have many friends. I was a "working ant". I loved nature, mountains and oceans. My father and the elders taught me to respect God "Man Above "and the lands of Hawaii.

I started working at nine years old selling newspapers and was a house-keeper at age eleven. I was told I had to work to support myself and help my mom and dad.

When I was a child, I thought I was a superhero. I thought I was like the Power Rangers.

I created things to get attention from my mother. I wanted her to see me. Some of you can relate to this. I wanted her to acknowledge me. She was also a "working ant". I was just like her.

My first memory was that I jumped off the roof of my grandparents' house with an umbrella thinking I would just glide through the sky like Mary Poppins. I was 7 years old.

I was a very spirited little girl. Wow, wrong plan! Thank God I still came out alive.

My second memory was with my mom. I was 9 years old; I was in the front passenger seat planning out a stunt. The plan was that I jump out of the car while she was driving, roll over, jump up and run next to her car. I jumped out alright and my mom was upset with me. Her reaction was "What is wrong with you? We must have a conversation with your dad". I had a little scratch, but I was fine.

My third memory was with my dad. I was at the pier helping my dad un-tangle a crab net rope. The rope was too long and tangled. My dad kept telling me to keep going backwards because the rope was long. I kept going backwards following my dad's instructions. To my surprise; Splash! I was in the ocean waters. Yes, I fell in!

It was fun, but I did not know the dangers around me. There were hammerhead sharks swimming close by. My father ran over to save me and a couple of men helped him pull me out of the ocean. My dad checked me from head to toe. He was amazed there were no bites and no damage to my body. I was not touched at all.

You see, God was protecting me from the harm throughout my childhood and adult life.

During my years in school, I was a quiet person. I spent my time with my friends and being an athlete. My school was a public school. My education was not the best. I had an English talking disability. I spoke our native language "Pidgin English". I had teachers who favored the quick learning students. You know what I mean. I was challenged to fights because I did not like lies and I didn't talk much. During that time of life as a student in my school you had to hold your ground and fight or be bullied. Not bragging, I thought I held my ground well.

My relationship with my parents was different. God bless them both.

My father was a man of adventure. He loved his cigarettes, beer and sashimi. He was a great cook. He loved being like James Bond. He was a perfectionist. He disliked people being late on any occasion. He was a military veteran. My athletic ability came from him. His friends called him Frenchie and the kids would call him coach. I remember his voice and his love for me driving him around the island. My father was a great cook and fisherman.

4

My mother was a serious, hard-working businesswoman. She was also a good cook. She was an operator for GTE and a real estate agent. On her personal time, she was a gardener. I got my work ethic from her. My mother was good in handling money. I got that from her also. I loved her, but I was not close to her. I felt I was not good enough in the things I did. I write this to let you the reader know why I felt this way. My mother would say to me, "You and I will never get along with each other". I did not know why. It stuck with me throughout my life. Parents be careful what you say to your children out of your distress.

I graduated from Pearl City High School in 1981. I continued working to help my family. I always stayed active in sports. I even tried figure fitness training.

I met a young handsome ex-marine mainlander and I fell in love. My father was tough on him. My father taught him to respect culture in Hawaii. My fiancée respected my dad. My fiancée asked my father if I could move to the mainland with him. I moved to the mainland and lived in Washington State for a while and later got married. We had a son a couple of years later. I was an overprotective mother due to some health complications with our son as he grew up. I wanted to have more kids, but there was difficulty in my marriage, and I lost our second child. I became thin and weak. This was a difficult time in my life. Thank God we had our son. I made sure my son was in a safe environment and that he had two parents that loved him very much.

I used to work for General Telephone (GTE). You folks of my time remembered the phone company. I also was a marine operator and information. I made a name for myself there. I enjoyed it. I was opening to the world and my mind and body was ready to learn this new life in mainland America.

Even though I was in Washington State I was homesick for Hawaii. God knew how to comfort me. He let me meet a special person. She gave me great words of encouragement that gave me the will to continue to stay in Washington State.

I ventured into a different world of social life. A friend introduced me to this "gathering". I was interested and on my days off I started taking classes. The subjects were about rocks, stones, readings, numbers, healing classes, dragons and psychic readings. I was also introduced to a meditation class originated in India. It was held at 7:00 p.m. I met many wonderful people. I remember there were people in a big circle talking about how they felt and they explained about the class. They would play beautiful meditation music. The leaders would go around and place their hands on your head and heal and give a blessing. One time I experienced seeing a beautiful elephant with jewelry and colors on it. I did not know what that meant. I saw a lot of different unexplained occurrences which I did not understand at that time, because I was without wisdom of God. It stuck with me and I kept coming to the gathering.

I did this for a couple of years. I met many people who have traveled to India, where this belief started.

I read books about the gurus, sages, the teachings and so on. I also recall listening to certain music that deals with certain consciousness. I went to a guru blessing in Portland, Oregon. I saw people in a calm and blissful moment.

This led thoughts back to my life in Hawaii.

You see growing up in Hawaii I was baptized Catholic and I did not understand the Catholic Church or the priest or any of it.

I would pray to God and the Catholic statues, all saints, Mother Mary and cherubs. I would also pray to the Hindu statues and there were many statues.

As I grew with this Spiritual Hindu group religion, I started receiving invitations to go to see The Avatars Temple Palace in India.

The leaders were supposed to have special gifts and people would go to receive blessings. People from all over the world would come for a blessing. They had monks and nuns. I have experienced seeing the Ohmers more than once. Ohmers were the "blessing givers." I remember they would decorate beautiful settings with either table or chairs with flowers and they played beautiful music to welcome the people coming to visit. I thought they looked at people's eyes and sent something to the receivers. I did not understand what exactly they were doing and why they were in this temple in Everett Washington. Were they taking something from us or were they receiving a part of us? Is this God or something else?

I remembered; You had to look at their eyes while they are looking at you for a couple of seconds. What I do know is that I would see lights or colors and I would feel vibrations from the spiritual person.

I really wanted to go to India and experience for myself the true meaning. All this sounded so wonderful. I met many people who have traveled many times to the temple palace and they came back enlightened, glowing, just in this bliss. I wanted to explore and understand what this was all about. I was not quite sure why I was drawn to this. A friend of mine helped me get my visa and travel arrangements to India and stay there for a short time.

I was working for a hospital for nine years. I was doing the job I liked, but I had more in me to experience in life. I told myself that I had to take this chance. I did it. I took my chance and asked for the first time to go on this month-long journey. I was denied. I did not give up.

I had to see what was calling me to India. This move was all about faith and trusting in God. I had to find out for myself. During this time, I got a divorce and my son moved to another state. I had all kinds of feelings inside me, sadness, frustration, anger, irritation, lack of forgiveness. I can go on, but you get the point.

These are challenges we sometimes face in our lives to give us the truth about ourselves. Let's get these words straight; I am not for divorce, but I had to face it, because it was on my plate to eat and I had to swallow it whole. This was a lesson while I prepared for the trip to India.

I was trying to take a month off from work to travel to India, but it was not happening. I even tried talking to the manager and supervisor but still I did not get the time off. This was not just about India; I also missed my son and I wanted to see him.

⟨⟩

My thinking about moving to Montana grew stronger so I had to make that move. Yes it was time to step out into the unknown.

I had been planning for months to take this leap of faith. Sometimes you must believe in what is in you and take the path less driven to make yourself alive again. I decided after praying on it and being patient. I gave my two weeks' notice to the hospital. This gave me time to get everything in order.

I took a couple of days off from the hospital, to get myself prepared. I rented a U-Haul and drove to Montana. I searched for an apartment in Montana. I was trying to be close to my son. I found an apartment on the same street as him. Everything was going according to plan.

I went back to Washington State and finished my two weeks at the hospital where I had worked for nine years. Those two weeks seemed to take forever, but I finally finished. The team gave me a farewell party. I was free and I was ready to get on the road.

Before I left for Montana, I stayed two nights at a hotel close to the highway I-5.

I remembered the day I left it was April 29, 2017.

I had everything in my car and at the storage unit in Montana. My apartment would be ready in three days. I stayed at Motel 6 in Missoula, Montana. This hotel was a great place to stay. The room was clean, and they had great customer service. The hotel was a futuristic style and personal.

I moved into my apartment on the 3rd floor. Wow, it was high! My neighbors were nice, and everyone was private. I was glad for that.

The moment of truth was in front of me. I needed to prepare for India. I had been waiting for this moment. Boy, I was overly excited. I had spoken my trip into existence and now I was flying from Missoula, Montana to Seattle, Washington.

I was on my way to Dubai via United Arab Emirates. I flew from Dubai to India.

This was an exceptionally long flight with a lot of time to reflect on my past and my dreams. It was fourteen hours and thirty minutes.

I was flying to Chennai, India. This is eastern India. When I arrived in Chennai, I checked into to the Taj Hotel. I love the people there, hardworking people, kind, very professional.

Even though I was being treated like royalty I saw a lot of poverty and poor people. This was quite different from America. Don't get me wrong, poverty is poverty no matter where you go.

After being in Chennai, India for a couple of days we had to transfer to the University Palace Temple. We were assigned a dorm room. This was different for me. I had not stayed in a dorm in years.

One of the "Ohmer's" placed me with a wonderful roommate, Sarah.

The staff was wonderfully kind and professional. We were serviced like we were royalty.

I have to say this; "WOW" There were lots of monkeys on the campus and dogs running around. The dogs had a different slim look and were light on their paws.

Every morning I woke up early excited for the day because I didn't want to miss out on anything.

On the grounds outside of the dorm door, the staff would draw beautiful artwork from their culture.

I am so grateful to have had this experience. Who knows when I will ever go back again? Oh, I will, with a different message, but let us get on with life and the many people I met in India.

I met so many people from all over the world. I woke up in the morning doing meditation before class started. I must remind you I am an early morning person. I could see that everyone came here for a reason. I wanted to see and witness for myself what was so special about this place.

The classes consisted of meditation, lessons from instructors, singing, dancing, and visiting the temple.

I got to see nuns and monks. I believe that I was meant to go there to witness for myself and see the truth. Sometimes when we are searching for something greater, we misunderstand the truth of who we are.

I have to say this because there is no one greater than God, the creator of heaven and earth. I believe my body was fighting certain rituals that were not holy. I remember when I was in the temple, they had these Pegasus slippers. I was in a deep meditation trance; the nuns had told us to move the slippers without touching them. Well, my hands grabbed the slippers and uncontrollably both hands were slapping the slippers hard on the tables as though to get the attention of what not to do. This is not right. I felt different while I was there. I felt OK but was in a different part of the world. What was I searching for?

We were in a room with many people from all over the world with translators to communicate if English was not your first language. Everyone was in a deep meditation with music and there was a TV scene with a picture of the person we came to see. I thought I would see him in person. They said he was not well. "Not well, what do you mean by that?" I paid a lot of money and traveled across the waters to see him. It was a lot of money to watch a TV screen. Everyone was meditating in a deep trance and I was setting far back trying to see the scene. Then suddenly, the person on the scene appeared not as a man, but a snake body with a human head. I looked around to see if any other person saw what I witnessed. Yes, you heard me. I looked around and no one was seeing this image. They were still chanting and meditating.

The best way I could describe this is the scene on the Conan movie when the high priest turned into a serpent while the people was meditating and spiritual feasting.

Again, I say I was looking at this person with a snake body. This was not what I expected to see. This was something different; dark, very dark. I kept it to myself for ten months. God opened my eyes to the truth so I could help tell the truth about these searches for power and identity. I had to see, so I could do my part to help the children of God come back to serving God Almighty.

It was time to return to the United States. We had a farewell party, said our goodbyes and I headed back home to Montana.

I was looking forward to returning to my new apartment. I still questioned myself for what I experienced, and I still was searching for God. I wanted to know him personally.

After I got back from India I went to work in Missoula, Montana.

I was hired at a local hospital called Montana Community Hospital. I worked in the surgery department. The staff was amazing. They worked as a family and had these great morning meetings. Everyone would express their feelings and frustrations for that morning at our surgery meeting before work started. The day would be a productive day and they would work as a team.

I loved the kind, caring, open hearted, hardworking employees with big hearts and this made my workdays productive also.

I enjoyed my personal time, I especially loved walking the trails and climbing Mount Sentinel. Climbing the mountain gave me this sense of closeness with God.

While living in Montana I started noticing I was losing a lot of weight. My skin looked different. I did not know what was going on in my body. Cancer was warning and calling me.

I received the word from God to return to Seattle and go back to my original job. Believe this; God and I had some words. I said, "God, I thought I was to stay for two years in Montana." His response to me was "No, it is time for you to return to Seattle." When God speaks you know his voice. It is a voice of certainty and truth and to the point.

I stepped out again with a leap of faith and returned to Seattle. When you receive your assignments, you obey God and trust him.

It was snowing when I moved from Missoula, Montana.

The thoughts running through my head were: "How am I going to do all of this alone?", "Move back to Seattle?". I thought I was alone. I was never alone. God was with me the whole time. There was a bigger reason for why I had to come back to Seattle.

I was rehired to my previous job. This was again right timing from God. The senior manager accepted me right away to return to work. I was blessed by God once again.

When I got back to Seattle God showed me three people to call so I would have a place to live. He assigned me to one of the families. In the family which I was assigned to live with, the husband had cancer. His name was Bob. There is a reason I wrote this. Unknown to me at the time, I was about to discover on May 15, 2018, that I had cancer.

I made an appointment to have a yearly checkup, through a close friend who referred me to an office. I remember while at the appointment, the medical assistant took my vital signs and told me the LPN nurse would be right in. During the time I first saw the nurse, she wanted me to come back in August for the physical. I was shocked and asked her "Hey what's up? I was paying for a physical now." I was paying. This was not right. The whole thing was confusing to me.

This is so amazing. It was clear as a bell I heard the word of God, "Vallyrie make another appointment with a medical doctor, at the same location right away". I obeyed and made that appointment with an internal medicine doctor.

At my appointment, my doctor had a nurse come in with him to help with the physical. I appreciated that respect. He gave me a full examination. The doctor also checked my breast and felt a lump. He ordered a mammogram right away. I made an appointment to have a mammogram for the next week. I knew something was wrong; you just know it. I felt so alone. I was in the city of Everett, Washington and there was no one I could confide in. When my time came for my mammogram, this was my longest day ever. I felt so bad because I was thinking about my son. After the mammogram was done, it felt like I had been waiting for three days in the waiting room. My goodness, it seemed so long! I had to see another person in a private room to go over the diagnosis. They told me, "Yes, you have breast cancer". I was diagnosed with cancer on May 15, 2018.

The doctor gave me the information and told me to schedule my first appointment with an Oncologist.

You must understand that everything was happening so fast; the information given to me was so strong and new. My mind was trying to concentrate, but the information was coming fast. Lord knows, I was trying hard not to cry. I was waiting to know what comes next. I needed to focus on the truth of this cancer and write down critical, crucial information to get right. It was a lot to take in and to accept. I have a son and ex-husband living in another state. No one here to talk to. I was alone and had to listen. Cancer was there pushing me to endure.

I took all the information in and went to the next step for healing. I had to be strong with faith and trust in God first. My faith and trust in God were being tested. I needed to get right with God first. Cancer is saving me now. Healing yourself starts with forgiveness. We will go over that later.

How could I break this news to my son? He was getting married on May 25, 2018. I called my ex-husband and let him know about my diagnosis with breast cancer. I did not want our son to know yet until after they got back from their wedding. I thought this would be the right time to let him know.

After my son's honeymoon I called my ex-husband and asked him to talk for me on a three-way line. I am so grateful that my ex-husband handled it.

When I mentioned to my son that I was diagnosed with stage one breast cancer he broke down in tears. My ex-husband (Shawn) took over the conversation. I thank God for that.

It was time to start healing. The early detection was critical; therefore, I said, "cancer saved my life". I am talking about myself. I needed to get my life back on track. It started with my faith.

The things I was doing against God 's will.

My idea for dealing with God was to be corrected. The meaning for this was beginning not to pray to statues, having rosaries, pictures of Jesus, angels, statues, dragons, Buddha, unicorns, fairies, idols of any kind. This was anything to do with false teachings. KJV Psalms 115:4-8.

I needed to get rid of all these false images and jewelry. Believe me, I did.

During this time, I was alone and wanted the company of a man. I did not want just any man. I did not want a macho man or muscular man. I wanted a holy man to teach me about the truth of God. We'd love God more than our human selves.

I planned and set forth to take this journey of faith to get healed.

Remember earlier in the book I told you about my friend Bob? I'm going to continue that and you will see how cancer started saving my life.

Before I had planned to move back to Washington state, I asked God "Where am I going to live once I return to Everett?" God had the plan set for me.

There were three people he wanted me to contact. The first one I thought was a close friend. He said no. The second person had other people staying with them. The last person was not what I wanted because I heard a loud voice in the background saying, "Who the h--l f--.ck is that?". God said "Yes, that is who you will stay with". Little did I know her husband had stage 4 prostate cancer.

At this time, I did not know I also had cancer. God sent me back to Seattle to get treated. I was living with this family. Little did I know God was preparing me for my own trials of faith, trust, redemption and truth. I was still praying to statues going to Catholic and Christian church and studying Hinduism.

Living with a family that is not my blood relations was uncomfortable. I had to learn about the pain of family difficulties, lies, deceitfulness, loyalty and hidden secrets that came to the surface.

Things of my past that I had suppressed, seemed to come forth inside my self being. I was staying with my friends, and I was paying rent of $550. There was no contract. What a blessing, huh?

I experienced the emotions with husband and wife, (pain, home unorganized, wife giving up and desiring to date other men even though her husband was dying from cancer). The home (meaning family) was a mess mentally and physically.

The room I rented was clean. I tried to keep to myself and not bother the landlords. I had a feeling the wife was spying in my room while I was at work. I would come to my room and find things out of place. This brought some childhood memories back.

Remember I told you about forgiving is the first step? I was not ready yet.

This learning experience, watching two adults so unhappy with one another was me. I could see and feel the husband's suffering and feel the wife's loneliness. The husband confided in me some personal things and he saw me as the daughter he never had. He wanted me to stay with him and not leave him alone with his wife. I felt I was put there to witness an event unfolding each day. God knows the truth and deeds in this family.

During my stay I gained a friend, Bob. He was suffering with cancer and I talked to him about God all the time.

I let him know how much God loves us. I wanted him to feel the same way I felt in learning the ways to Christ Jesus.

At that time, I was still struggling with the graven images thing. Catholicism was embedded in my mind.

There are many verses in the bible that identify this as a dislike from God. I had a picture of Jesus, just like so many other families in this world.

Some people are in denial; some were taught wrong and some just don't care.

I did not know these pictures were not Lord Jesus Christ. They were created to take our trust and respect, to keep us true children of God blind from the truth of his desire for us to be one with him the true God.

Generations to generations have been lied too and taught wrong. I don't know if this was taught this way on purpose or accidentally. I write this to make us understand the truth and why I was suffering with cancer.

I watched Bob's body deteriorate daily and the pain and suffering he went through. He wanted to travel to other parts of the world for a healing. He had already been to India and studied naturalism.

I was placed with this family to understand what was going to happen to me.

Through all this searching and trying to find my way, God has been there all this time.

He allowed me to stay with friends that helped me and in return I helped them.

My friend Bob did not believe or trust chemo or radiation; his approach to cancer being natural with no harsh chemicals. I was there for an important mission to help Bob through these difficult times and for myself.

Some of us humans are searching for something greater, better and more powerful than what we are. There is nothing greater than God Almighty. How incredibly blind I was to think God needed help.

My searching into this unknown for something greater was high, risky and dangerous to my soul. Cancer was the result, warning me. We must remember our hearts and minds are built on confusion if we are without God.

The devil's responsibility is built on confusion to make us hate God. His duty is to make us not believe in God. I was so easily fooled by the devil. I see now, that was all false.

We must remember that God is a jealous God. He wants us to serve him and only him. I want to go to heaven not hell.

God gave me time to come back to him. Cancer was my intervention and only God knew the beginning the middle and the end of my life cycle.

While on my journey back to God a friend of mine at the hospital where I was employed, told me that a healing prophet was coming to Pasco, Washington. My friend's family was from Paris, France. I decided to drive to Pasco from Everett, Washington following my friend. There were many people who came to see the prophet from all over the world. This was a three-day event.

My friend Bob who I was living with was in hospice care now. I would visit him daily before I left for Pasco, Washington.

I always prayed for him hoping to see him when I got back. I was staying at the Red Lion hotel in Pasco.

Everyone was so kind helpful and just wonderful. This was my first time at the meeting. The first day at the event and there were many people from all over the world. People came for medical reasons, to be saved, to remove spirits, to be blessed, etc.

I have never experienced anything like this. I did not know what to expect. What I do remember was seeing the prophet walking back and forth on the stage and holding his big blue bible cover with bright gold pages shining close to his heart as he walked back and forth looking at the audience. When it was time, they would line up people from row to row.

We could hold a picture of someone to be blessed, even when they were not physically there. The prophet was either tapping people's forehead, chest, or casting out spirits and healing them.

I thought again this was the work of God. This experience was coming through God. When it was my turn, I could not decide if I should show my son's picture or someone else.

When the prophet saw me, he touched my head and I fell backwards. Then suddenly, I heard, "Vallyrie get up". You must understand I was battling self-identity. What I mean is I changed my name and I was searching for true love, (family issues as a child feeling not good enough, not smart enough.) I heard Lord Jesus speak "Get up Vallyrie." A voice that I will never forget. He called me by my real name. No fake name. No made-up name. It was my birth name.

Your name is important to God because it is in the book of life. God knows your real self.

You see, I had been searching for my self-identity and after that moment I knew who I was. I sat up.

I came back the next day. Remember, this was a three-day event. On the second day later in the evening the prophet was still blessing people, healing and casting out spirits. I noticed he was looking tired and sweating. I started praying for him asking God to fill him up with energy and light, because there were a lot of people waiting their turn to be blessed. I kept praying. People were singing and glorifying God.

Then suddenly, I went into a deep prayer while standing. I felt this presence of holiness around me.

What I saw was me away from Pasco to somewhere else like a river where there was a person baptizing people.

You couldn't see the faces. Every time the prophet would cast out a spirit, I would see with my eyes closed that this person or persons were being baptized in a river. I did not realize that everyone was sitting and I was the only person standing. One of the security people from the church told me to sit down or I would have to leave. I tried to explain to him, "You don't understand I am praying for the prophet". Another young man said, "I understand. Could you please sit down and do it quietly?". I felt humiliated. I started to cry and said, "Lord Jesus they don't understand". So, I closed my eyes and kept praying. During this praying suddenly I saw a white wall going round and round faster. It kept going up and up to the heavens, and it would not stop and there was gold mounted all around this white wall.

I asked, 'God is this heaven?' And it stopped. Thank you, Lord Jesus.

I left the auditorium while the service was still going on. Two people who were inside the service with me asked me what happened. I told them.

While I was walking to my car after service, late at night, I saw a dark car with no headlights, heard an engine getting louder and louder. The sound of the engine began to become loud, fearful and threatening. I prayed that I would get to my car safely and travel back to my hotel with no one following me. Thank you, Lord Jesus, I made it back safely. I felt something inside me as if I was being directed to leave early the next morning to get back to the hospital to see my friend Bob.

When I got back the nurses informed me that my dear friend Bob who called me a daughter, had passed away an hour earlier.

I stayed and prayed for him. It was time for me to move again.

I asked another friend if I could move in with her and her family because I did not feel comfortable where I was. Her family agreed to let me stay with them. Each situation I was in was teaching me about holy and unholiness. My friend had a problem with me talking about God. I loved God. Her family did not feel comfortable, so I tried not to get anyone upset or uncomfortable.

No one at my jobsite knew I had been diagnosed with breast cancer yet. I called my director and manager and told them. I wanted everyone at my jobsite to know just in case I needed help or assistance. I let my friend know that my first treatment of chemo was coming up. Before that I had to have my port put in. I did not feel this was happening until that fateful day getting my port implanted. My manager was so kind to take me to my appointment to have my surgery for placing my port above my right breast. The port is placed under the skin. That device is used for chemotherapy.

The surgical staff in the surgery room were amazing. I trusted them because I am a part of the surgery team. I was wheeled on the gurney into the surgery room. At that moment when they moved me from the gurney to the surgical table, I began crying. It really hit me. This is really happening. This is real. Cancer was here and I was fighting to cure it. I was really healing myself. The surgical staff was so supportive of me.

I decided to stay in a hotel for three days after my first chemotherapy to have peace and calmness around me during my first treatment.

I began to question myself (What did I do wrong?). I was praying to God and still making mistakes, praying to what I thought was right. I was praying to God, statues, false pictures Indian gods. They have many statues and gods. Praying to a person who calls themselves something that does not exist; this was not God, but the enemy. I say it again cancer saved my life. You are wondering how.

When I was going through chemo God was opening my eyes, mind, heart and soul to the truth. God was trying to save me. I did not quite understand just yet. I was learning about God, for God is a jealous God. Praying to gods and to statues and using rosaries is all wrong, a sin. The statues cannot hear you. All of this is not God at all. I learned the hard way and that is why I am writing this book to educate people to come clean with God. KJV Matthew 7:23.

As a child I was conditioned to pray to statues and so were my parents and generations before that.

This is so important for all children of God to clean out their house and garages with statues, idols, fake images and pictures of Jesus Christ. There is no Caucasian, black, Asian, Indian Jesus Christ. Our Lord God is not flesh and bone but a spirit. John 4:24 God is a spirit; and they that worship him must worship in him in spirit and in truth.

Exodus 20:3-5, Thou shall no other Gods before me. Thou shalt not make unto thee any graven image, or and likeness of anything that is in heaven above, or that is in the earth beneath, or that is in the water under the earth. Thou shalt not bow down thyself to them, nor serve them; for I the Lord thy God am a jealous God visiting the iniquity of the fathers upon the children unto you the third and fourth generation of them that hate me.

Leviticus 26:1. Ye shall make you no idols nor graven image, neither rear up a standing image, neither shall ye set up any image of stone in your land, to bow down unto it; for I am the Lord your God.

You see when you get this lesson called Cancer it de roots all beliefs that are not of God. This was a revelation to me. I was shocked to know those pictures, statues, rosaries, offerings (food, incents, handmade images) we have in our churches, homes, temples are not of God. The pictures in our bibles, history books of Jesus are not the Lord Jesus Christ at all. It meant well for us, but they are not the real Lord Jesus Christ. I began to study how the imagery of Jesus Christ started in the USA. It was like a movement with a plan. It started in the USA and parts of Europe. Images of Christ were put in place for certain controls and misguidance.

The confusion, hatred and misguidance caused other nations to put the imagery in their ways, such as the black Jesus Christ and the Asian Christ. They are not the Lord Jesus Christ either.

There was a famous picture drawn by an American artist, called Warner Sallman. He was from Chicago, Illinois. He was known for Christian religious imagery. His famous picture was the "Head of Christ". 500 million copies were sold.

He partnered with two Christian publishing companies. It was then published throughout the world for personal reasons not God's way. There are arguments about the way Christ Jesus looked. The bible gives certain descriptions in the scriptures about the Almighty God. KJV Revelation1:14-20. You have to read that with understanding also.

There were no pictures of Jesus the Christ during his human life on earth. Just imagine how many souls were lied to about God and Jesus and his appearance. I was one of those souls. I did not know about the real Lord Jesus, but I still wanted to go to heaven and get right with God.

Sometimes you want your flesh to win in this life we live. This is another reason cancer saved my life. Cancer made me tough and mentally strong. It made me see the way is not always easy but with a strong will you can overcome all things. That was cancer with a touch of the Holy God inspiring me the whole way. I was preparing for death also. If the Lord Jesus was going to take me, I wanted to be pure hearted and soul cleaned.

During my personal times of reading and going through chemo I would reflect on my life and have conversation with God, as though he was sitting or standing with me just listening to me. I said, "Lord it would be so nice to talk to a human person to help me to understand about life and everything that is happening, teaching me your ways and helping me to see you as the true savior of my life."

I cried out for I was lonely and wanted company, but I wanted a particular company. I prayed and asked God to send me a holy man.

"Lord, just to have someone that loves you more than life." I waited for some time and of course when it was not happening. I said, "Lord Jesus when is this holy man coming?" God replied, "Vallyrie, you must be patient for this person is busy on another assignment".

"Yes Lord, is this person with someone?" "Yes child." My sad response, still waiting, said "OK Lord Jesus, thank you."

The mystery of God's healing began to teach me about people and their feelings and attitudes while helping the needy. Cancer was that guideline for my way to understand the issue in front of me.

I remembered a bad experience while checking into the surgery department. This would affect me and my lessons in forgiveness. I had this uncomfortable feeling in my port placed above my right breast. I started having discomfort and pain. I decided to ask someone about my port.

It began with this employee. I don't know if she was having a bad day, but it was not a professional one. This employee called me to the side and took me to a room close to the front desk for checking in for surgery. In this room this employee said to me, "Who do you think you are coming here trying to get a free service?" I don't know if I reminded her of another patient, but I was not in the mood for this type of treatment. My quick Hawaiian upbringing came out of my mouth at her. "What is your problem?" I asked. I told her. "I was hurting where they placed the port". She responded in a rude way "Well let me see it". I just wanted to leave. I allowed her to inspect the port. She was very cold, rude and unprofessional. After I got away from that negativity, I felt I had to do something about this, because it was not just for me, but for the other cancer patients who were coming there for service and treatment.

I asked the front desk who this employee was. They protected her and would not give me the name. I took the next step and called my director and told her what had happened. This is not professional at all. She was not happy about this situation and treatment of patients. She contacted the director of that department.

Months passed. I finally saw this person and I knew her name. I didn't say a word to her. I had to forgive her and I just prayed to myself "Lord please help this woman," she does not know that what she does and says can cause harm to patients going thru cancer and surgery". "She needs you Lord Jesus". Cancer has it way of making right right. I forgave her and my healing continued.

You see, God was with me always. Through all of this, cancer had its role in healing my soul. If you are listening to cancer, it will make you fix your life and become truthful and honest.

Cancer can save your life. While going through treatment, I was not afraid because I knew God was with me. Every time I came in for treatment, I saw anger, sadness, depression, loss and fear from other patients. I always tried to talk about God with people and patients like me. I just wanted them to know that God is real. His healing hand was there for us to grab and believe that we are healed.

God is amazing in how he uses certain things to make us grow in his wisdom. God came to me again, because he knew it was time for me to have my own place. I heard God in my spirit leading me and guiding me to find my own place to stay. The place I lived at was too much stress and my friend's father wanted me out. I was on a mission to find a new place.

Remember everyone, I was listening to the word of truth, finding a place for me to stay. On this day the side effects of the chemo treatment were kicking in. The chemo had some strong side effects. I had to empty out my stomach two to three times at the other hospital. This is what chemo does to you. It will either make you vomit or have diarrhea. I was getting drained out with dehydration.

I heard the voice again. "Vallyrie you are close. Go around the block again, by the other hospital campus." I followed the directions and I saw a For-Rent sign.

I said, "Oh my God, Lord this is where another co-worker lives. All this time you were trying to tell me my place was near and all I had to do was open my eyes in you Lord Jesus. I was so distracted by my stomach and diarrhea." When I saw the for-rent sign, I was so excited. I heard the voice say "Park your car Vallyrie. Write down the number and call it right now."

The distraction began again with my upset stomach. I prayed that my stomach would calm down because I had to go to the bathroom again.

I called the number and the landlord answered. I told him I knew someone that lives in his apartment complex. I told the landlord I was there waiting for him to see the apartment. He said he would be there in five to ten minutes. At the same time my stomach was getting worse. I knew I could not leave. He showed up and looked at me with concern because I was very pale. I explained that I was going through chemo, and I needed to find a place. He said, "I have sixty applicants who want this place." He confided in me that his wife went through cancer treatment.

He asked me "Do you want it?". I responded, "By the way I haven't seen it yet and didn't hear how much the rent was." He asked me and I said "Yes, can I look too?". "Yes", he said. When I saw the place, I knew this was it. It is a basement that in the 1920's the nurses and the nuns lived in. This basement is large with a garage and washer and dryer. The landlord said I could move in tomorrow. The day was a Sunday. There was something he had to do before he gave the keys. He needed to show this place to a gentleman from out of town. To make this story short the other person did not accept the place, so I did. The rest is history. This was another miracle from God. I am still living here, because it was a true blessing from God.

I worked during my chemo. I worked fulltime four ten-hour shift days on and three days off. I chose to work because I am single and divorced.

I was inspired by a nutritionist, who was giving a class for cancer patients and family. She was teaching us to eat correctly during the fight against cancer. She said this and it stuck with me. "We have coworkers who work in the emergency department and receiving chemo and they are working full-time". Coworkers would ask me why I am working. My response to them: "I got bills to pay. I can't give up." I chose to work to show brothers and sisters that you can work and still be productive even while you are fighting cancer. I wanted to stay busy and not feel sorry for myself.

After my first chemotherapy I felt fine. I had three days off.

I returned to work and the effects of the treatment hit me like a "ton of bricks". One morning at work I felt very tired and weak. I went to the Bistro bathroom. The Bistro was a coffee shop in our hospital. It was on the first floor of the hospital. While I sat on the toilet, my vision was seeing yellow all around in my stall. I believe this was a warning. My breathing becomes short. I felt like I was going to pass-out. I felt weak and limp. I knew I had to get help. I had to get out of the bathroom! My heart rate dropped. I felt I could not breathe. I tried to stand up and open the door of the bathroom stall. I saw my yellow marker fall to the floor and then I passed out. I do not know how long I was down. I heard the voice of God, "Vallyrie get up". "Come on". "Get up slowly". "Come on". "You need to get help." My heart was beating slowly as though I was dying, but with the grace of God pushing me to survive and having faith, I made it out the bathroom holding the wall. I sat at the table by the Bistro. Suddenly, I saw security and told him, "I am a cancer patient please take me to the emergency room". I was wearing my scrubs. He went to get me a wheelchair. Shortly after that conversation I saw one of my supervisors. She took me to the emergency room. They gave me an IV and watched me for observation. I needed liquids and my blood pressure had to be normal. I was in the emergency room for 2-3 hours.

They took me to an observation room and the nurse assigned to my room was amazing. Everyone on that fateful day was so kind from their heart. It was as though God put all of them in position to help me on that day.

I broke down and cried while I confided in the nurse when she talked to me. I was in great thought and worried about my son.

I found out during our conversation that she was from Montana also. She made me feel comfortable with the words she spoke to me. I let her know that I lived alone and no family was close to me for all of them are out of state.

She asked me if I had a bed. I told her I sleep on a cot. She and her husband got me a bed and delivered the bed with all the trimmings. This made a big difference for my sleeping, rest and recovery. She didn't have to, but I accepted the offer. They wanted to do more, so they offered me friendship and let me spend time with them one afternoon after work.

She took me to the Everett Port Marina on a sailboat. I mean, this just does not happen to me! I went on the boat with the nurse, her husband and a friend they had invited. They bought a huge watermelon and cut it up and we sat and ate watermelon on this beautiful sailboat on the waters. She provided Gatorade for me, because of my dehydration.

I began to see the light that God was showing me during my suffering with cancer. The tool of redemption was cancer.

Cancer saved my life. God gave me time to get right. I did not know if I was going to die. I just wanted to be right in my lifestyle.

I stopped praying to fake statues, rosaries, stopped going to these meditation classes and worshiping people who think they are Godlike and they
are not. These false people think they have power and they give themselves
false names of powers.

In my life on this journey of truth, only God has all the power. I had to get
right with God first and put God first before anything or anyone. Cancer
was his net for me to give all to God.

Remember the first and most powerful step to healing cancer is forgiving?
I had to forgive family members and friends who trespassed against me. If
I did not forgive them, how do I expect God to forgive me?

Forgiving is in stages and God knows when you have finished them. You
know it also because you are at peace with yourself.

The next step to forgiving is forgiving yourself. You must do this, because
if it is not accomplished you cannot obtain the Holy Ghost.

You make a promise to God and you don't ever break it ever. He knows
your true self. There are consequences if you break your promise with God.
I say this to all my cancer patients and other ill patients. I even say this to
the family members and friends who make promises to GOD to heal their
in-laws and friends.

Going through all of this was to help me to understand that I took the
wrong path, but God never left me. He wanted me to figure things out
and take his path. It seems to be a lonely path, but God was with me all
the way.

If I did not take the leap of faith to move to Montana, then travel to India, I would have continued sinning, thinking the path I was traveling was ok, when it was not.

In the end sooner than later, I would have ended up a lost soul and death would have been waiting for my bones without a good soul to meet the presence of God.

Going through the chemo and radiation kept my faith, strength, truth and trust strong. You do not realize how blessed you truly are until you experience faith and love for God. You have love and hunger for God Almighty.

Going through cancer brought my soul closer to God. Believe me, the devil wanted me to hate God and turn against him. God was there every step of the way and showing me, "as I was among you so shall you do as I do live as I lived." Holy is the way. I enjoy hearing Lord Jesus' voice every single day. It is so amazing that God gives me love sometimes more than I can handle but I take it anyway.

Cancer led me to being prayerful in all things. I pray for the world, children, world leaders' families, neighbors, co-workers, homeless, the list goes on. I thank God for all he has done for me. I tell God I love him very much.

He allowed me to get cancer. I think about brother Job in the bible and how he was tested. He gave his love to God only. Cancer brought me back to God. You must understand cancer is not the end, but a great path to God. He could have taken my life more than once. You see God has saved my life as a child and adult. We the children need to listen to God's voice. He always warns us when to leave, where to go, who to deal with, and how to fight troubles. They could be our fault or a lesson from God.

Jesus Christ is always warning us, but it is up to us to listen and obey God. Please do not be stubborn and hardheaded and think you know it all. Google is not God. It's a tool that God allowed us to use, but Cancer was a warning for me and the greatest tool from God to me.

Remember, God will get you through your weakness. If you listen to God and allow him in your mind and your heart, spirit, soul you are at peace with yourself. The devil wants your soul and will try to get you through your weakness. His tool is to make you feel angry, depressed, have anxiety, sadness and loss of will. The list can go and on.

My love for God is glorious, beautiful and wonderful. I cannot get enough.

I thought I was going to die. God never said I was going to die. He did not give me permission to die yet. I was preparing for the worst. When I found out I had breast cancer, I began to get rid of personal things. My house was very bare. I did not want to be a burden to my son.

During my process, I met people that hated and blamed God, or hated the cancer, swearing and cursing it. When I saw these lovely people in pain like me, I approached them with reasons from God. "You must ask yourself why? Not why me? Do you understand? The Almighty God was calling you. You were too busy to listen or having a good time or it is a generational curse passed on, which need to be broken by you accepting God as your savior and living right on to you."

Remember, God is trying to have the children of earth come back to him. You must realize and understand that God loves us. We are his children. Remember he is a forgiving God. When we are angry at our illnesses, diseases and physical ailments, God is trying to get our attention. Stop! Stop!

Take that short time to listen! It will save your life. Mostly it will save your soul.

Your body is the temple of God so it can't be corrupted with foolish ideas and religions and acts of sin. This is true for me.

This is a wake-up call. You start to look at life in a different eye, not like before. I wanted to do right before God because he knows our hearts. God knows the beginning and the end.

We know this by KJV Isaiah 46:9-10 states, Remember the former things of old: for I am God, and there is none else; I am God, and there is none like me, declaring the end from the beginning, and from ancient time the things that are not yet done, saying, my counsel shall stand, and I will do all my pleasure:

I want the children of God to get right too. I also did not know that I needed to get baptized correctly, because I was baptized as a Catholic not knowing that in the bible it never said to be Catholic or any other religion. It only showed Christ saying to be holy like him. Nothing, just holy. Live a righteous life. The King James version bible states, in 1 Peter 1:16, "Because it is written, Be ye holy; for I am holy.

It is crucial and important to be baptized. You must be baptized correctly by a pastor that has received the Holy Ghost. His message of baptism must be stated as in Acts 2:38; "Then Peter said unto them, Repent, and be baptized every one of you in the name of Jesus Christ for the remission of sins, and ye shall receive the gift of the Holy Ghost.

This means that you need to submerge (go under the water). You must be baptized by a Holy Pastor filled with the Holy Ghost.

It does not mean:

- You get baptized with the saying" I baptize you in the name of the father, son and the Holy Ghost – who's name. He has a name.

- Pouring or sprinkled water on the head, the Roman Catholic Church simply asserted the symbolism of the of the bath, is preserved by a ritual infusion of water.

- You join a church, or you say the so-called sinner's prayer. "I am a sinner, and I ask you for your forgiveness I believe you died for my sins and rose from the dead. I turned from my sins and invite you to come into my heart and life I want to trust and follow you as my Lord and savior

- Someone on TV says "Just touch the tv screen and repeat after me, I'm a sinner please come into my life save me wash away my sins. Call this 1-800 number to speak with someone.

Here is my story of my baptisms. I thought I was on the right path of salvation. I embraced all this fake sacrificial act of giving my soul to God. I thought my body was cleaned from the sin that ate my body inside and out. Can you believe this? I got baptized three times. Why?

1st time — Catholic Church; hey pour water on my head and mumble some words I did not understand.

2nd time — Christian Church; they ask me for my name and what I wanted to say before they dunk me in the water. Wrong again.

3rd time — got baptized in Portland by the First Church of our Lord Jesus Christ. I heard the message of Our Lord Jesus. I accepted it. I was baptized according to Acts 2:38. The minister said "I baptize you in the name of Jesus Christ". I was submerged in the water. I got baptized correctly. Now I tarry for the Holy Ghost.

I say it loud and clear; Cancer saved my life with the grace of God.

God is real and angels are too. Remember demons and devils are real also. God created all the universe, the heavens and the earth.

One last personal experience happened in my home. I was still fighting cancer. I was sleeping in my guest room. I was awakened suddenly. My quilt was covering my head. I moved the quilt and I saw a man lying next to me. I jumped out of the bed and reached to my left side as if I was reaching for a sword. Oops that is right, I do not have one! I don't know why I reacted that way. I looked at this man in my bed. He was tall, big with black curly hair and rosy cheeks, and his eyes were wide- open looking up. Amazingly, I was not scared, I just wanted to know who he was. He did not say a word. He just looked up at the ceiling then slowly his body started to disappear. The last thing to leave was his eyes. They went up and out through the small window in my guest bedroom straight out towards the light of the sky.

These things make you know that there is a God and we must believe in him. Angels do exist for they are here to protect the children of God.

Psalms 34:7 states, "The angel of the Lord encampeth round about them that fear him and delivereth them". I gave this chapter and verse to explain this experience. I learned this after I began that relationship with God. I was still learning the ways of God.

I felt it was a spirit, but at that time I carried some fears of the unknown, because of my previous spiritual beliefs. I had doubt so I called a Christian church and talked to a pastor. I explained what I had seen to him. I invited him to come to my home and bless it. I was happy he accepted my request to bless my home. "Thank you, Lord Jesus, a pastor is coming". He was incredibly careful before coming into my home.

The pastor prayed, wow his prayer wasn't short. Oh no. He prayed long strong beautiful prayer with the words I thought were from God Almighty. I am grateful.

Lessons to be learned: All preachers are not holy or called by God to preach. They are book smart, but not Holy Ghost smart. The meaning of this is that God calls holy preachers to do his bidding for souls. I learned that there are men who are great motivational speakers using the bible as their way of making a living. I can go on and on about this, but this is for a later book.

I have a personalized license plate. I am going to share the story with you. While I was going through chemo, I heard the word of truth say "Go and get a personalized license plate. This license plate will read, "Dove 777" This license will have an eagle background. This license plate will be a warning for believers and non-believers to get right with God. I asked, "How Lord"? he said, "When brothers and sisters see your license plate, they will feel different. They may feel happy, sad, angry and curious".

I visualized God playing a large screen of my life. I had to get right with God. We call this the Book of life. Revelations 20:11-15

Remember earlier I asked God about waiting for a holy man? God is a mysterious being and he does things in his time. At my jobsite we had a new person coming into a department. Whenever we have a new employee, we would introduce ourselves to him or her in group meetings. Everyone introduces themselves in the circle. The new employee's name was Abraham. When it came to my turn I said, "my name is Vallyrie." A friend next to me said, 'Vallyrie, Abraham said your name twice. My interest peeked my thoughts "Vallyrie look on the assignment board and see where Abraham workstation is. Go to him and introduce yourself." I'm shy and wondering, here goes nothing; I responded, "OK Lord Jesus". I looked and noticed that we were both scheduled to work in assembly. I walked up to him and said, "Hi Abraham my name is Vallyrie. If you need help, please just let me know." The way he looked at me was so shocking. He just stared at me with his mouth slightly open. I had no idea why he was staring. I thought I had something on my scrubs.

Little did I know why, until he explained to me. There are brothers and sisters out there who hear the word of truth and are on assignments. This assignment could be helping others get right with God. Abraham was on his new assignment. Remember I asked GOD for a holy man. Abraham's assignment was to come to Seattle. He did not want to come Washington. He had to follow GOD. When you receive your assignment from God, you must be obedient.

Abraham revealed to me that he already knew my name. What? He had a vision of me. Beautiful. How can this be? He loves God, trusts, and believes in him. He had a vision of me. Abraham spoke to me in this deep voice of his" I was in his apartment wearing a (Mumu) spring dress, sitting on his bed eating his cereal. I said, "sure, aha". Suddenly he said, "Didn't you ask God for a holy man?" I said, "Who are you? Really, are you an angel in disguise?" That won't happen because angels are not flesh. I was amazed. All of this is true. I asked and he delivered.

I said to God I wanted someone who lives for GOD, who loves God and someone who can explain to me about the scriptures, holiness and so much more. We are still studying the word of God together. We both have to submit to God fully. We have missions to finish and souls to save.

Every day is a lesson with God. We are children of God. We are not perfect like God. Working to be holy takes practice, obedience, devotion, trust, and faith in God at all times of the day.

We must always do it God's way, and when we do wrong, we must repent and ask for forgiveness from God. Remember, God sees our hearts. Be truthful and God will reward you. Like I said, God has been with me since I was in my mom's womb. God has never left me. The net was cancer and it was the tool to my salvation and return to holiness.

I left God by believing in made up religions and statues and ideas of man.

Today I am a true God believer. I love God and no other gods. I am grateful to God for opening my eyes of truth and I hearken to the word of truth, which was described to me through cancer.

Now I know the reason I had to go to India and see what I saw on the screen. I had to see the devil and how he has tricked many people from finding out about God.

Satan has tricked many souls to forget God and his love. We must strive to get the word to all people trying to find their way. God and Satan are fighting for our souls. We are God's children and the devil hates God's children because they love God.

As I said, everyone must get right with God. The enemy wants to bring fear. What do you prefer heaven or hell? I prefer heaven. Everyone will have their day of judgement with God. Devils or demons are real. I am glad that God made me who I am today. I love God and I will continue to serve God until my last breath. Amen. Hallelujah.

I end this book with a beginning to another book, the book of Ephesians (chapter 5:1-7)

Followers of our Lord Jesus Christ must live according to the teachings of the bible. It did not say we would not make mistakes and not fear or fall. It says live this way and know you have a redeemer in the truth which is God our Lord and Savior Jesus Christ.

I will say it again. This is written from some of my personal experiences. I will write other books and they will go more into detail more about God's teaching me how to be a holy woman.

Cancer made me decide what path to travel. Be holy and God is holy. Let your illness or problems, lead you to holiness, as it did to me. Lord Jesus will forgive you. God forgave the murderer, Apostle Paul who went on to preach the words of God to the gentiles. Christ Jesus forgiveness is waiting for you to accept.

Lord Jesus has forgiven us. When you accept Christ Jesus, don't be hard on yourself. Forgive yourself and live righteous. Holiness is not easy, It's the pathway for your soul to be with God forever.

This was written for you, who are in the world of cancer. You have worried your mind and spirit out. Your mind is thinking, why me. You are confused and ready to give up. Listen to what I must tell you. It was God's will for me to learn from cancer. You see, cancer destroyed evil in my soul and body. It was the work of cancer that allowed me to see the light hidden in the darkness of my soul. I had cancer all the time, but it was not to be given to me as a disease, but as a living lesson that God is with me. It was given to me for me to find my way back to him. This is written for those who are seeking for the truth and want to stop running.

We can fool ourselves with time. We can fool our friends part of the time. We can't fool God at any time. He is truth and he created us with a DNA for us to know him. We may ignore him, forget him or try to say he does not exist, but the DNA is still there.

The word of God is your way, whether you live or die. It is the book of truth and holy scriptures to guide you back to God almighty. He loves you no matter what you think of him.

I leave these words for my cancer friends. Search truly with an open heart and God will find you. He is waiting for you to learn your lesson and get right with him. You will be healed according to his will and your faith. Healing will come. Whether it means cancer was destroyed or your soul was saved by Lord Jesus with your death. Remember Cancer is a tool that can help or destroy you. It's your choice heaven or hell. Your self-will is what God gave you to think for yourself. Make that important decision. He awaits your answer.

Remember, sometimes hard lessons make wise leaders in Jesus Christ. I am one of those leaders for women who serve God in truth. I reach out and help the needy and I give them some spiritual guidance. I will always witness to all who are sick and ill. Cancer is my joy, pain, sadness, but most of all it was my lesson from our all mighty Lord and Savior Jesus Christ.

Isaiah 53:5 (KJV) tells us that he died for our sins and took a major beating for our illnesses. Each strike of the whip was for our healing. I say if you believe this you are ready for the journey of healing.

God's love, mercy and peace be unto you and may God give you the chance and faith you need to come to him and accept him so he can restore your salvation.

Lord Jesus Christ is waiting for you to decide. Lord Jesus chose to save me with cancer. Cancer was the tool that saved my life and my soul. It gave me the alerts I needed to come back to GOD. I am thankful that cancer came when it did so I would not be lost from God's love.

Cancer left an imprint in my soul. "**GRWG**" which is my company name "Get Right with God".

You are called and God's glory and salvation are in your hands. Be not the one who turns him away. Lord Jesus loves you and his power is almighty. Follow Acts 2:38 and start your life again in the truth of God message. I did and I am working on doing the will of God and that is to be holy for he is holy. I say again, it takes self will to be holy and a commitment to God so that you are willing to sacrifice your flesh to worship him. If cancer did not come my way, I would still be serving the devil and doing all these crazy things created by man. On the other hand, I probably been dead with no way to salvation. Cancer saved my soul. Your illness can do the same thing. God is waiting for you.

I end this book with a prayer:

Our Great father in Heaven you are the light of the world. Be with all that reads this book of decision making and soul searching. Your true words are our light and your love is our home.

We care for all that is true, which is you Lord Jesus. We honor and glorify you with all our heart, soul and mind. We thank you for the pains and illnesses you have allow us to experience.

We will take them as a tool to get right with you. Thank you, Lord God and give us the will to continue move forward even in our darkest hour. I thank you for giving me the strength to write this book to show others there is a true way of love and life which is called holiness. I thank you Lord Jesus for cancer and the road it took me on, testing my will and faith in you Lord God. I pray that this book touch even just one soul and give them the joy of you Lord Jesus Christ. You are with us always and you have never left us.

I pray all of this to our Lord and Savior Jesus Christ

Amen